MY Mum bakes AWESOME cakes!

Published in 2014 by
Speechmark Publishing Ltd, Sunningdale House, Caldecotte Lake Business Park,
Milton Keynes, MK7 8LF, UK
Tel: +44 (0) 1908 277177 Fax: +44 (0) 1908 278297
www.speechmark.net

002-5932/Printed in the United Kingdom by Hobbs the Printers.
British Library Cataloguing in Publication Data
A catalogue record for this book is available from the British Library

ISBN 978 0 86388 998 1

MY Mum bakes

AWESOME
Cakes!

Jo Johnson

Illustrated by Lauren Densham

Speechmark

NOTES FOR PARENTS

"Parents who have a diagnosis of multiple sclerosis (MS) often ask "How can we talk to our children about MS?" The answer is straightforward: you can talk to them about MS in the same way that you talk to them about all other aspects of your lives as a family.

Honesty is vital; children always know if things are being kept from them, and consequently imagine things to be much worse. They need to know that MS is a disease but that it is not something that can be caught or made worse by their behaviour.

Your child needs reassurance that it is not a terminal disease and they need to be given information about the most common symptoms.

They need an opportunity to ask questions and to feel that it is all right to ask questions at any time in the future. As they get older they will want more information as their cognitive ability improves.

It is my opinion that adults often overload children with too much information about the technical details of MS, the meaning of the name, why it causes the symptoms it does and how the brain and spinal cord are impaired. A few children like this kind of information but most children want to know how it will impact them, will Mum still be able to take them to ballet or do the cooking, can dad still go swimming and kick a football.

This book has been designed so that children of between five and eight can read it independently. However, ideally it should be used with an adult to facilitate discussion about all aspects of family life and to enhance general emotional wellbeing. The book deliberately makes MS one of many things going on for this small group of children because for most children MS is only one of many issues in their family life.

The story is intended to emphasise that all families are different, with their own strengths and weaknesses and different experiences. MS is another experience that some people encounter and others do not.

Use the book as a template to enable you to create your own family book that is personal to your family life. Together, create a book that includes the names and adventures of your family and the positive and negative experiences that MS creates.

Jo Johnson

Consultant Neuropsychologist

Other books by the same author include:

"My Parent has a Brain Injury" ... a guide for young people
Aimed at older children and teenagers

In the Neurology Series:

My Dad makes the Best Boats
For younger children who have a Dad with a brain Injury

My Mum makes the Best cakes
For younger children who have a Mum with a brain Injury

My Dad builds Awesome boats!
For younger children who have a Dad with MS

Grandpa Seashells
Talking about Dementia

Leah is six today. She is very excited.

Her Mum has made her a cake that looks like a princess castle.

Holly, Alex, Isaac and Joshua come to Leah's party. They love the cake.

"Your Mum makes the best cakes. I wish my Mum could make such great cakes," says Holly.

How old will you be on your next birthday?

The next day Leah and Alex are playing in the garden.

Leah's Mum sits in the deck chair and watches them run about and play.

"My Mum is always too busy to watch me play. I like your Mum," Alex tells Leah.

Leah's Mum laughs. "I have to sit," she says, "I get very tired."

What games do you like to play?

Leah is learning to read.

Every evening before she goes to bed, her Mum listens to her read.

Leah's favourite book is about Biff and Chip.

Her books are funny, and Leah and her Mum laugh a lot.

What do you like to do with your Mum?

Today is sports day. Leah, Alex and Holly's team win the egg and spoon race. They are very excited.

Holly's Mum runs in the Mummies race but Leah's Mum has MS so she can't run in the race. Leah and her Mum cheer for Holly's Mum and clap when she wins.

What things does your Mum find difficult?

The children go back into school and the Mums and Dads go home.

"Why can't your Mum run?" asks Holly.

"She has MS," Leah says.

Alex thinks she's said, "My Mum has a mess." Leah thinks that's funny.

The girls giggle. "Boys are so silly."

Leah tells her friends that MS is a disease that makes her Mummy's legs go wobbly and makes her tired and sometimes very sad.

Do you talk to your friends about MS?

After school Leah and her friends are at running club.

"Why don't you have wobbly legs like your Mum?" Alex says.

Leah laughs. "You can't catch MS or get it from your Mum. It is not like a cold or chicken pox!"

The girls think boys are very silly. Alex wishes he could run as fast as Leah.

Do you like a particular sport?

Leah is eating her dinner. It's her favourite: mashed potato, sausages and carrots with lot of gravy. She is thinking to herself.

Mum is upstairs injecting the medicine she takes for MS. When Mum comes down Leah says. "At school I told Alex that you can't catch MS."

"That's right," Mum answers.

"But if you can't catch it, how did you get MS?"

What's your favourite food?

"That is a good question but nobody really knows why some people get it."

Dad says, "The good thing is that lots of doctors are working very hard to find out why so they can help people like your Mum."

"I hope they find out soon," Leah says.

Mum smiles: "So do I."

Do you have any questions about MS?

Holly is having tea with her Mum. She is sad. She is worried that Leah's Mum might die of her disease.

Holly's Mum smiles and gives her a hug. "MS does not kill people Holly. It just makes some things difficult. Leah's Mum gets more tired than other Mums. Sometimes it is difficult for her to walk and sometimes her eyes go funny and she can't see very well."

Holly feels happy that Leah's Mum can keep cooking such great cakes.

What makes you feel worried or sad?

Dad is grumpy. He has had a busy day at work. Leah's little sister Ellie has got paint on the chair.

Dad shouts at her. Ellie cries and Mum tries to pick her up.

Mum's legs go wobbly and she has to put Ellie back down.

Do your Mum's legs go wobbly sometimes?

Leah shouts at her sister. "You have made Mum's MS bad by being so naughty!" Leah feels upset.

Dad says, "Nobody can make Mum's MS bad or good. Mum is having a bad day because of the MS, not because we have all been grumpy." Dad brings out some of Mum's homemade cake.

They all eat it and everyone feels happy again.

What makes you feel happy?

Today is Mother's Day. Leah's teacher is called Miss Underwood. Leah and Holly like Miss Underwood. She is fun.

The teacher gives them all a piece of paper with hearts on it.

"Write something nice about your Mum," says Miss Underwood.

Did you do something for your Mum on Mother's Day?

Holly writes, "I love my Mum, she can run fast."

Alex writes, "My Mum reads me stories; I love stories."

Leah writes, "My Mum makes awesome cakes."

They all stick their pictures on a big poster. The poster says, "We love our Mums!"

Write something nice about your Mum.

Today is Leah's birthday, she is seven. Holly, Alex, Ella and Lucy come to her party. Mum carries out a pink cake in the shape of a princess castle.

"Wow," says Alex, "your Mum makes awesome cakes!"

"I know," smiles Leah, "she is the best Mum!"

Did you have a cake for your birthday?

MY mum bakes
AWESOME
cakes!

Activity pages

Spot the Difference

Can you spot the 13 differences?

Wordsearch

B	S	W	F	Z	N	A	U	S	L	C	G	M	P	M
A	E	S	V	A	I	U	P	K	J	Y	N	O	L	U
L	I	T	E	X	T	A	R	R	Y	N	I	O	A	S
A	F	R	A	N	S	I	M	S	E	B	R	D	T	C
N	F	T	K	M	B	Y	G	U	E	X	R	S	J	U
C	A	G	G	U	E	M	R	U	G	B	U	S	S	L
E	E	N	K	L	H	O	U	E	E	R	L	G	J	O
B	R	A	I	N	L	U	K	N	L	V	B	E	T	S
M	X	N	N	O	R	U	E	N	G	C	M	L	Y	K
S	E	A	G	E	V	R	E	N	G	C	S	Y	R	E
O	E	I	S	S	E	N	I	Z	Z	I	D	U	O	L
P	S	Y	N	L	V	K	M	V	Y	I	L	V	M	E
T	H	J	E	F	L	V	E	R	T	I	G	O	E	T
B	G	X	V	A	Z	R	F	D	L	K	C	S	M	A
J	X	B	W	T	T	O	A	J	T	A	A	C	J	L

ataxia	legs	neurologist
balance	memory	neuron
blurring	moods	numbness
brain	muscle	nurse
dizziness	musculoskeletal	spasm
eyes	myelin	vertigo
fatigue	nerve	walking

All about me...

I don't like

My Name is

These are the people in my family

Colour the shape below in your favourite colour

The colour of my eyes is

Draw your favourite food on the plate below

Draw your house in the cloud below

Draw a picture of your family

All about my Mum...

Here are some facts about
my Mum...

Name ....

Hair colour ....

Eye colour ....

Birthday ....

Favourite animal ....

Favourite sport ....

She really doesn't like...

Does your Mum have a
favourite thing she often
says? Write it in the speech
bubble below!

Draw a picture of your Mum
doing her favourite thing in
the box below

Think of something you could do
to make your Mum smile and
write it in the cloud below

Spot the Difference Answers

1 Extra balloon on string (left)

2 extra stripe on breadstick pot

3 extra crisp in bowl

4 extra wobble line on green jelly

5 lemonade cap colour

6 different shape on baloon string (right)

7 line on pocket of Reuben's trousers

8 extra line under table

9 Leah's hair missing colour in one bit

10 extra pepperoni on pizza

11 extra star on banner

12 extra cup in stack

13 line on Reuben's teeth

For further information and support on
Multiple Sclerosis, please visit the websites below:

www.mstrust.org.uk

www.shift.ms

www.mssociety.org.uk